GEOMETRY
WORD PROBLEMS:
NO PROBLEM!

MATH BUSTERS WORD PROBLEMS

Rebecca Wingard-Nelson

NEED MORE PRACTICE?
free worksheets available at
http://www.enslow.com

Enslow Publishers, Inc.
40 Industrial Road
Box 398
Berkeley Heights, NJ 07922
USA

http://www.enslow.com

Library of Congress Cataloging-in-Publication Data

Wingard-Nelson, Rebecca.
Geometry word problems : no problem! / by Rebecca Wingard-Nelson.
    p. cm. — (Math busters word problems)
Summary: "Presents a step-by-step guide to understanding word problems with geometry"—
Provided by publisher.
Includes bibliographical references and index.
ISBN 978-0-7660-3368-9
1. Geometry—Juvenile literature. 2. Word problems (Mathematics)—Juvenile literature.   I.
Title.
QA455.5.W5546 2012
516.0076—dc22
                          2010006295

Printed in the United States of America

062010 Lake Book Manufacturing, Inc., Melrose Park, IL

10 9 8 7 6 5 4 3 2 1

To Our Readers: We have done our best to make sure all Internet Addresses in this book were active and appropriate when we went to press. However, the author and the publisher have no control over and assume no liability for the material available on those Internet sites or on other Web sites they may link to. Any comments or suggestions can be sent by e-mail to comments@enslow.com or to the address on the back cover.

♻ Enslow Publishers, Inc., is committed to printing our books on recycled paper. The paper in every book contains 10% to 30% post-consumer waste (PCW). The cover board on the outside of each book contains 100% PCW. Our goal is to do our part to help young people and the environment too!

Illustration credits: © Comstock/PunchStock, p. 9; © Digital Vision, p. 32; Shutterstock.com, pp. 5, 7, 11, 12, 13, 14, 17, 19, 21, 22, 23, 25, 26, 27, 28, 29, 30, 35, 37, 38, 40, 43, 45, 47, 49, 50, 53, 54, 56, 57, 59, 60.

Cover Photo: Shutterstock.com

Free Worksheets are available for this book at http://www.enslow.com. Search on the *Math Busters Word Problems* series name. The publisher will provide access to the worksheets for five years from the book's first publication date.

Contents

Introduction

When you see a picture on a wall that
appears to be crooked, you're living in a word problem!
Math is everywhere; you just might not realize it all the time
because math isn't always written as a math problem.

This book will help you understand
how geometry is used in word problems.
The step-by-step method can help students, parents,
teachers, and tutors solve any word problem.
The book can be read from beginning to end
or used to review a specific topic.

① Problem-Solving Tips

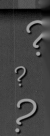

How do I start? What do I do if I get stuck?
What if the answer is wrong when I check it?
Word problems are hard for me!

Get Involved!

You can watch a swim meet and see swimmers racing across a pool, but if you want to learn to swim, you must get in the water. Solving math problems is not a spectator sport. You may first watch how others solve word problems, but then you need to solve them for yourself, too. Go ahead, jump in!

Practice!

Even the most gifted athlete or musician will tell you that in order to play well, you must practice. The more you practice anything, the better and faster you become at it. The same is true for problem solving. Homework problems and class work are your practice.

Learning Means <u>Not</u> Already Knowing!

If you already know everything, there is nothing left to learn. Every mistake you make is a potential learning experience. When you understand a problem and get the right answer the first time, good for you! When you do NOT understand a problem but figure it out, or you make a mistake and learn from it, AWESOME for you!

Questions, Questions!

Ask smart questions. Whoever is helping you does not know what you don't understand unless you tell them. You must ask a question before you can get an answer.

Ask questions early. Concepts in math build on each other. Today's material is essential for understanding tomorrow's.

Don't Give Up!

Stuck on homework? There are many resources for homework help.
- Check a textbook.
- Ask someone who does understand.
- Try looking up sources on the Internet (but don't get distracted).
- Read this book!

Getting frustrated? Take a break.
- Get a snack or a drink of water.
- Move around and get your blood flowing.
  Then come back and try again.

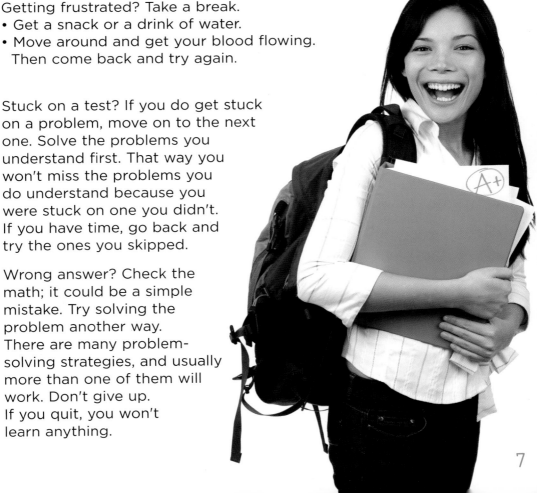

Stuck on a test? If you do get stuck on a problem, move on to the next one. Solve the problems you understand first. That way you won't miss the problems you do understand because you were stuck on one you didn't. If you have time, go back and try the ones you skipped.

Wrong answer? Check the math; it could be a simple mistake. Try solving the problem another way. There are many problem-solving strategies, and usually more than one of them will work. Don't give up. If you quit, you won't learn anything.

② Problem-Solving Steps

What steps can I take to solve word problems? If I follow the steps, will I be more likely to get a correct answer? Will I have less trouble finding the answer?

Problem-Solving Steps

Step 1: Understand the problem.
Step 2: Make a plan.
Step 3: Follow the plan.
Step 4: Review.

Step 1: Understand the problem.

Read the problem. Read the problem again. This may seem obvious, but this step may be the most important.

Ask yourself questions like:
Do I understand all of the words in the problem?
Can I restate the problem in my own words?
Will a picture or diagram help me understand the problem?
What does the problem ask me to find or show?
What information do I need to solve the problem? Do I have all of the information I need?

Underlining the important information can help you to understand the problem. Read the problem as many times as it takes for you to have a clear sense of what happens in the problem and of what you are asked to find.

Step 2: Make a plan.

There are many ways to solve a math problem. Choosing a good plan becomes easier as you solve more problems. Some plans you may choose are:

Make a list.	Guess and check.
Draw a picture.	Work backward.
Use logical reasoning.	Solve a simpler problem.
Use mental math.	Use a number line or graph.
Use a model.	Use a table.
Write an equation.	Use a proportion.
Use a formula.	Use previous knowledge.

Step 3: Follow the plan.

Now that you understand the problem and have decided how to solve it, you can carry out your plan. Use the plan you have chosen. If it does not work, go back to step 2 and choose a different plan.

Step 4: Review.

Look over the problem and your answer. Does the answer match the question? Does the answer make sense? Is it reasonable? Check the math. What plan worked or did not work? Looking back at what you have done on this problem will help you solve similar problems.

③ Basic Geometry Terms

? ? ? ?

Four friends are standing on a circle. What is the total number of line segments that can be drawn to connect any of the two friends?

Step 1: Understand the problem.

Read the problem. What is a line segment? **A line segment is part of a line. It has a starting and ending point.**

What does the problem ask you to find?
The total number of different line segments that can be drawn to connect any two friends on the circle.

What information do you need to solve the problem?
The number of friends.

Step 2: Make a plan.

line segment

Let's draw a picture.

Step 3: Follow the plan.

Draw a circle. Use a point on the circle to represent each friend. Start at any point. Draw a line segment from that point to each of the other three points.

Move clockwise to the next point. Draw a line segment to each of the two points that are not yet connected.

Move clockwise to the next point. Draw a line segment to the point that is not yet connected.

Geometry Terms

point: A place in space. A point has no size, so it can't be measured. A point is usually represented by a dot on a page.

line: An unending set of points that are on a straight path. Lines extend forever in two directions. Lines are shown by drawing a piece of a line, and putting an arrow on each end to show that it keeps going. Lines have no thickness and no length, so they can't be measured.

plane: A flat surface that extends forever in every direction. A plane is a flat edge, like a piece of paper, but a plane has no thickness.

The next point clockwise already is connected to the other three points.

Count the number of line segments.

You can draw 6 different line segments.

Step 4: Review.

Does the answer match the question? **Yes. The problem asks for a number of line segments.**

Using the picture, can you see any other line segments that are possible? **No.**

④ Lines

Zach told Tina to meet him at the corner of Harding Street and Genner Road. Using only the map, decide if this is possible. Explain.

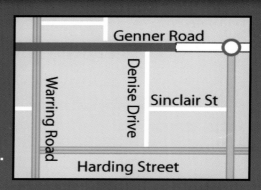

Step 1: Understand the problem.

Read the problem. Restate the question in your own words.
Is there a corner where Harding Street and Genner Road meet?

What information do you need to solve the problem?
A map showing the roads in the problem.

Step 2: Make a plan.

Find the street and road on the map. Decide if they intersect.

Line Relationships

Intersecting lines are lines that meet. The point where the lines meet is called the **point of intersection**.

Perpendicular lines are intersecting lines that form four right angles (90°).

Parallel lines are lines that are in the same plane and never intersect. They are always the same distance apart.

Step 3: Follow the plan.

Look at the map. Find Harding Street. Find Genner Road.
How are Harding Street and Genner Road related?
They are parallel.

What does parallel mean?
Parallel means that they go in the same direction and never cross.

It is not possible for Zach and Tina to meet at the corner of Harding Street and Genner Road. The street and road do not intersect because they are parallel.

Step 4: Review.

Part of the answer is to explain why they can't meet. Did you explain the answer? **Yes.**

Is is possible that the street and road meet further along somewhere that is not shown on the map?
Yes, but the problem says to use the information on the map.

⑤ Rays and Angles

Kadin was riding his skateboard, jumped in the air, and turned to go back in the exact direction he came from. What was the angle of Kadin's turn?

Step 1: Understand the problem.

Read the problem. What does the problem ask you to find?
The angle of Kadin's turn.

What information do you need to solve the problem?
The problem tells you that Kadin turned so that he was going in the exact direction he was coming from. This is enough information to solve the problem.

....

Step 2: Make a plan.

Let's use a picture to understand what happens in the problem. Then use what you know to decide the angle of the turn.

....

Step 3: Follow the plan.

Draw a ray showing the direction Kadin is riding his skateboard. Let's draw the original direction ray in red. Think of the vertex, or point on the ray, as the spot where Kadin is when he turns. The arrow part of the ray shows the direction he is going.

vertex

ray

Rays and Angles

If you cut a line into two pieces, the results are called **rays.** A ray only goes on forever in one direction. The other direction has an endpoint.

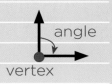

Angles are formed where two rays, lines, or line segments intersect. The point of intersection is called a **vertex**. You can think of angles as turns. The size of the turn is measured in degrees.

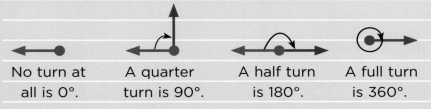

| No turn at all is 0°. | A quarter turn is 90°. | A half turn is 180°. | A full turn is 360°. |

When Kadin turns, he is going back in the direction he was coming from. Let's draw a ray showing the direction Kadin was coming from in blue.

The rays form a half turn, which has a measure of 180°.

The angle of Kadin's turn was 180°.

....

Step 4: Review.

Does the answer match the question?
Yes, the problem asked for the angle of Kadin's turn.

Is there another way you could solve the problem? **Yes. You may have known without a picture that this turn was 180°.**

⑥ Angle Classification

The inner tip of a flower petal forms a 20° angle. If three of the petals tips are put together, what kind of angle is formed by the three petals?

Step 1: Understand the problem.

Read the problem. Is there anything you do not understand?

What does the problem ask you to find?
The type of angle formed by the three petals together.

What information do you need to solve the problem?
The measurement of the angle at the tip of the petal.
You also need to know the different types of angles.

Step 2: Make a plan.

Let's write an equation to find the total measurement. Then decide what kind of angle is formed.

Angle Classification

Angles are classified by how they relate to 90° and 180°.

Acute angles measure less than 90°.
Right angles measure exactly 90°.
Obtuse angles measure greater than 90° and less than 180°.
Straight angles measure exactly 180°.
Reflex angles measure greater than 180° and less than 360°.

Step 3: Follow the plan.

The measure of angles can be added just as any other number. When two angles are put together to share a side, the measure of the large angle is the sum of the two smaller angles.
For this problem, there are three angles added, so you can multiply the measurement of one angle by three to find the total.

measure of one angle **times** **number of angles** **is** **total measure**

20° × 3 = 60°

The measure of the angle formed by the inner tips of three petals together is 60°.

What kind of angle is a 60° angle? **Acute.**

The angle formed by the inner tips of three petals together is an acute angle.

Step 4: Review.

Does the answer match the question?
Yes. The problem asked for a kind of angle.

Does the answer make sense? **Yes.**

Is there another way you could solve this problem? **Yes. You could have drawn a picture to understand the angle size.**

⑦ Angle Relationships

Angle 1 has a measure of 48°. Angle 1 and angle 2 are supplementary angles. What is the measure of ∠2?

Step 1: Understand the problem.

Read the problem. Is there anything you do not understand?

What does the problem ask you to find?
The measure of ∠2.

What information do you need to solve the problem?
You need to know the measure of ∠1 and the definition of supplementary angles.

Step 2: Make a plan.

You know the sum of supplementary angles, and you know the measure of one of the angles. You can use subtraction to find the measure of the other angle. Let's subtract.

Related Angles

Adjacent angles are angles that share a vertex and a side.
Congruent angles are angles that have the same measure.
Complementary angles are two angles with a sum of 90°.
Supplementary angles are two angles with a sum of 180°.

Step 3: Follow the plan.

Supplementary angles have a sum of 180°. Subtract the measure of ∠1 from 180° to find the measure of ∠2.

180° − 48° = 132°

The measure of ∠2 is 132°.

Step 4: Review.

Does the answer match the question?
Yes. The problem asks the measure of ∠2.

Check your answer. Add the measure of the two angles.
132° + 48° = 180°

The angles formed by the trunk of this cheerleader's body and one of her arms are adjacent supplementary angles.

⑧ Intersecting Lines

Angle 1 and angle 2 are vertical angles. If the measure of ∠1 is 68°, what is the measure of ∠2?

Step 1: Understand the problem.

Read the problem. Is there anything you do not understand?

What does the problem ask you to find?
The measure of ∠2.

What information do you need to solve the problem?
You need to know the measure of ∠1 and the definition of vertical angles.

Step 2: Make a plan.

Use what you know about vertical angles.

Linear Pairs and Vertical Angles

When two lines intersect, they form four angles. The four angles are related in special ways.

Any two adjacent angles formed by intersecting lines are called a **linear pair.** Linear pairs are supplementary angles, since they form a straight line. The sum of their measure is 180°.

Any two angles that are across from each other when two lines intersect are called **vertical angles**. Vertical angles are congruent.

Scissors can form vertical angles.

The blades form one of the angles, and the handles form the other.

Step 3: Follow the plan.

Vertical angles are congruent. They have the same measure. When you know the measure of one of the angles, you know the measure of the other. Angles 1 and 2 are vertical angles, and you know the measure of ∠1.

The measure of ∠1 is 68°, so the measure of ∠2 is also 68°.

Step 4: Review.

Does the answer match the question?
Yes. The problem asks the measure of ∠2.

If angles 1 and 2 were a linear pair, and the measure of ∠1 was 68°, how could you find the measure of ∠2?
A linear pair has a sum of 180°. You can subtract to find the measure of ∠2.

180° − 68° = 112°

⑨ Polygons

a. Which road sign does NOT show a polygon?
b. Name the shape of the crosswalk sign.

Step 1: Understand the problem.

Read the problem. What is a polygon? **A polygon is a plane figure with sides that are all line segments.**

What does the problem ask you to find?
Two things. First it asks which one of the signs is not a polygon. Second, it asks the shape of the crosswalk sign.

Do you have all of the information you need to solve the problem?
Yes. You have pictures of all the signs.

Step 2: Make a plan.

Use the picture and what you know about plane figures to answer the questions.

Plane figures are figures that lie in one plane and are made up of curves and line segments.

Step 3: Follow the plan.

The first part of the problem asks which sign is not a polygon. Plane figures with curved edges are not polygons. Which sign has curved edges?

The No Bicycles sign is not a polygon.

Polygons

Polygons are named by the number of sides and angles they have. Some common polygons are:

A **triangle** has three sides and three angles.
A **quadrilateral** has four sides and four angles.
A **pentagon** has five sides and five angles.
An **octagon** has eight sides and eight angles.

The second part of the problem asks the name of the shape of the crosswalk sign. The sign has all straight edges (line segments), so it is a polygon. Count the number of sides to find the type of polygon. **The sign has five sides.**

The crosswalk sign is a pentagon.

Step 4: Review.

Did you answer both parts of the problem? **Yes.**

The crosswalk sign is a pentagon. Is it a regular pentagon?
No. Regular polygons have sides that are all the same length and angles that all have the same measure. The crosswalk sign has a longer edge on the bottom.

⑩ Perimeter

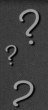

Jamie and Tera want to hang a string of lights on the perimeter of the roof of a lifeguard tower. The edge of the roof is a square with 8-foot sides. How long does the string of lights need to be?

Step 1: Understand the problem.

Read the problem. What does the problem ask you to find?
The perimeter of the roof of the tower.

What information do you need to solve the problem?
The length of each side of the top of the tower.

Is all of the information that you need in the question?
Yes. The problems tells you the top of the tower is a square with 8-foot sides.

Step 2: Make a plan.

You can find the perimeter of the roof by adding the length of each of the four sides of the roof.

Step 3: Follow the plan.

A square has four sides. Each side of a square is the same length. Add the length of each side to find the sum.

8 feet + 8 feet + 8 feet + 8 feet = 32 feet

The string of lights needs to be 32 feet long.

Step 4: Review.

Does the answer match the question?
Yes. The problem asked for a length.

Is there another way you can solve this problem?
Yes. A square is a regular polygon. The perimeter of a regular polygon can be found by multiplying the number of sides by the length of each side.

<u>number of sides</u> <u>times</u> <u>length of each</u> <u>side</u> <u>equals</u> <u>perimeter</u>

4 × 8 ft = 32 ft

Perimeter is the distance around a figure.

⑪ Quadrilaterals

This rectangular piece of stained glass has been marked to cut. What type of quadrilateral will be formed when the glass is cut?

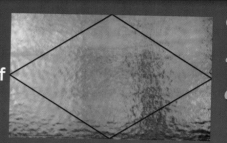

Step 1: Understand the problem.

Read the problem. What is a quadrilateral? **A quadrilateral is a polygon with four sides.**

What does the problem ask you to find?
The new shape of the glass after it has been cut.

What information do you need to solve the problem?
The types of quadrilaterals.

Types of Quadrilaterals

Quadrilaterals are classified by how their sides are related.

A **trapezoid** has exactly one pair of parallel sides.
A **parallelogram** has two pairs of parallel sides. The parallel sides are congruent, or equal in length.
A **rhombus** is a parallelogram with four congruent sides.
A **rectangle** is a parallelogram with four right angles.
A **square** is a rectangle with four congruent sides.

Step 2: Make a plan.

You are shown the shape in the picture. Compare the shape to the types of plane figures you know.

Step 3: Follow the plan.

Are any of the sides parallel? **There are two pairs of parallel sides. This makes the figure a parallelogram.**

Do any of the sides appear to be congruent? **Yes. All four sides appear to be congruent. This makes the figure a rhombus.**

Does the figure have any right angles? **No, there are no right angles. This means the figure is not a rectangle or a square.**

The quadrilateral formed after the glass is cut is a rhombus.

Step 4: Review.

Does the answer match the question?
Yes. The problem asked for the type of quadrilateral.

Can the quadrilateral also be called a parallelogram?
Yes. It is a parallelogram. The figure is both a rhombus and a parallelogram. Rhombus is a better term because it is more specific.

⑫ Triangles

Jewel cutters classify triangles when they describe the cut of a stone. Look at this jewle. Classify the triangle shown on the outlined face by its angles and sides.

Step 1: Understand the problem.

Read the problem. Is there anything you do not understand? What does the problem ask you to find?
The classification of the triangle by angles and sides.

What information do you need to solve the problem?
The picture of the triangle being classified and the types of triangles.

Step 2: Make a plan.

Use what you know about triangles to classify the one shown.

Step 3: Follow the plan.

The problem tells you to classify the triangle simply by looking at it. This means you do not need to use any measuring devices.

The triangle needs to be classified by angles and by sides. Look at the angles first. All of the angles appear to be less than 90°. What kind of triangle has all acute angles?

An acute triangle.

Triangle Classification

By Angles:
An **acute triangle** has three acute angles.
A **right triangle** has exactly one right angle.
An **obtuse triangle** has exactly one obtuse angle.

By Sides:
An **equilateral triangle** has three sides with the same length.
An **isosceles triangle** has two sides with the same length.
A **scalene triangle** has no sides of equal length.

Now look at the sides of the triangle. Two of the sides appear to be the same length, but the third does not. What kind of triangle has two side that are the same length?

An isosceles triangle.

The face of the jewel is an acute isosceles triangle.

Step 4: Review.

Does the answer match the question?
Yes. The problem asked for the triangle classification.

Can you check your answer? **Yes. You can use a protractor to check the angles and a ruler to check the length of the side.**

⑬ Angle Sums

Ann and Eva are on the beach watching Marcus surf. When a triangle is drawn connecting the girls and Marcus, the angle at Ann's vertex measures 90°.

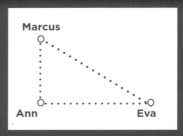

The angle at Marcus vertex measures 60°. What is the angle measure at Eva's vertex?

Step 1: Understand the problem.

Read the problem. Is there anything you do not understand? What does the problem ask you to find?
The angle measure at Eva's vertex.

What information do you need to solve the problem?
The angles at the other vertices.

Step 2: Make a plan.

The points where Ann, Eva, and Marcus are located form a triangle. Use a sketch to clarify the problem. Draw three points and label the angles.

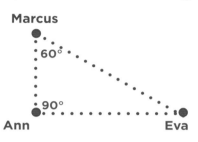

The sum of the interior angles in a triangle is always 180°.

The interior angles of the triangle have a sum of 180°. You know two of the angle measures and need to find the third. Use mental math to find the missing angle measure.

Step 3: Follow the plan.

It is easy to add the sum of the two angles you know because they both end in zeros.

Think: 6 + 9 = 15, so 60 + 90 = 150

Subtract the sum of the two angles from 180° to find the missing angle.

Think: 18 - 15 = 3, so 180 - 150 = 30

The missing angle is 30°.

At Eva's vertex, the angle measure is 30°.

Step 4: Review.

Does the answer match the question?
Yes. The problem asked for an angle measure.

Check the answer. Do the three angles have a sum of 180°?
90° + 60° + 30° = 180° Yes.

Polygon Angle Sums

? ?
? **What is the sum of all the interior angles of a baseball diamond?**
?

Step 1: Understand the problem.

Read the problem.

What does the problem ask you to find?
The sum of the interior angles of a baseball diamond.

Do you have all of the information you need to solve the problem?
No. You must know from other sources that a baseball diamond is a four-sided figure.

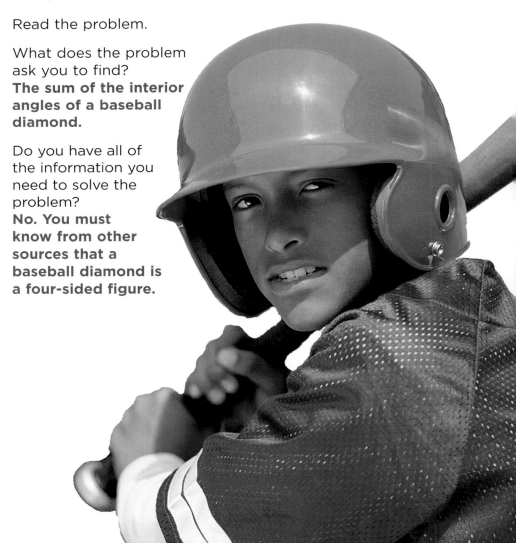

Step 2: Make a plan.

Draw a picture. You can use what you know about the sum of the angles in a triangle to find the sum of the angles in a quadrilateral.

Step 3: Follow the plan.

Draw a baseball diamond. Draw a diagonal to divide the diamond into two triangles. A diagonal is a line from a vertex to any non-adjacent vertex.

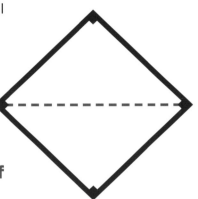

Each triangle has an angle sum of 180°.
There are two triangles.
Add 180° for each triangle.

180° + 180° = 360°

The sum of the interior angles of a baseball diamond is 360°.

Step 4: Review.

Does the answer match the question?
Yes. The problem asked for a sum of angle measures, so it should be a measurement in degrees.

Each of the angles in a baseball diamond has the same measurement. What are the measurements of each angle?
There are four angles, so each measures 360° ÷ 4 = 90°.

Ariel has two poles for the front end of her tent. They are each 5 feet long. Can Ariel set up the triangular end of her tent so that the bottom side is 12 feet wide?

Step 1: Understand the problem.

Read the problem. Draw a sketch to help you understand and picture the problem.

What does the problem ask you to find?
If Ariel can make a triangle for the front of her tent that is 12 feet wide at the bottom.

Do you have all of the information you need to solve the problem?
Yes, you know the length of the two side poles.

Step 2: Make a plan.

For three lengths to form a triangle, the sum of the two shortest lengths must be greater than the longest length. Add the two shortest lengths and compare the sum to the longest.

Triangle Inequality Theorem:

The sum of the measures of any two sides of any triangle is greater than the measure of the third side.

34

Step 3: Follow the plan.

The lengths of the two known sides are 5 feet and 5 feet.
Add these two sides.

5 ft + 5 ft = 10 ft

To form a triangle, this sum must be greater than the third side.
Is 10 feet greater than 12 feet? **No.**

No, it is not possible for the bottom of Ariel's tent to be 12 feet wide.

Step 4: Review.

Does the answer match the question?
Yes. The problem asked you to answer a yes or no question.

Why can the tent end not be 12 feet wide at the bottom?
A drawing can help make this clearer.
Draw a line to show the tent bottom as 12 feet wide. Draw two 5-foot-long poles that point straight up. Picture the pole tops moving down and inward.

5 ft   5 ft

12 ft

What happens?
The tops of the poles never touch.
The poles would end up on the floor of the tent, with a 2-foot gap in the center.

⑯ The Pythagorean Theorem

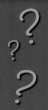

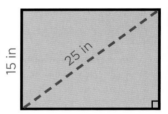

? ? ? ?

Laptop computers are advertised by the length of the diagonal of their screen. An advertised 25-inch laptop is 15 inches tall. How wide is the screen?

Step 1: Understand the problem.

Read the problem. What does the problem ask you to find?
The width of the screen.

What information do you need to solve the problem?
The diagonal and height of the screen.

Step 2: Make a plan.

Computer screens have rectangular faces. Drawing a diagonal on the screen forms a right triangle. You can use the Pythagorean Theorem to find the missing measurement.

15 in   25 in

Step 3: Follow the plan.

The height of the screen is one leg of the triangle, *a*, and the diagonal forms the hypotenuse, *c*.

Write the Pythagorean Theorem, then substitute in the values that you know.

$$a^2 + b^2 = c^2$$
$$15^2 + b^2 = 25^2$$
$$225 + b^2 = 625$$
$$b^2 = 400$$

What number when it is multiplied by itself equals 400? **20, so b = 20**

The screen is 20 inches wide.

a^2 means a multiplied 2 times, or a x a. This is read as "a squared."

The Pythagorean Theorem

The Pythagorean Theorem says that the sum of the squares of the two leg lengths is equal to the square of the hypotenuse. This is usually written as $a^2 + b^2 = c^2$, where a and b are leg lengths and c is the hypotenuse length.

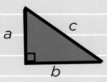

Step 4: Review.

Does the answer match the question?
Yes. The problem asked for a measurement.

Check the answer by substituting the values into the Pythagorean Theorem.

$$a^2 + b^2 = c^2$$
$$15^2 + 20^2 = 25^2$$
$$225 + 400 = 625$$
$$625 = 625$$

Lance is covering his vegetable garden with a mesh sheet to help stop weeds from growing. How many square feet of mesh does he need for a rectangular garden that is 5 feet wide and 4 feet long?

Step 1: Understand the problem.

Read the problem. Is there anything you do not understand?

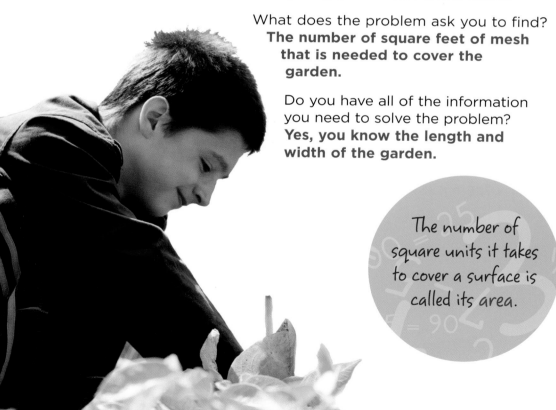

What does the problem ask you to find?
The number of square feet of mesh that is needed to cover the garden.

Do you have all of the information you need to solve the problem?
Yes, you know the length and width of the garden.

The number of square units it takes to cover a surface is called its area.

Step 2: Make a plan.

You can draw a picture of a garden that is 5 feet wide and 4 feet long. Use the picture to count the number of square feet in the garden.

Step 3: Follow the plan.

Draw a rectangle that is 5 feet wide and 4 feet tall. One square foot is one foot wide and one foot tall. Count the number of square feet.

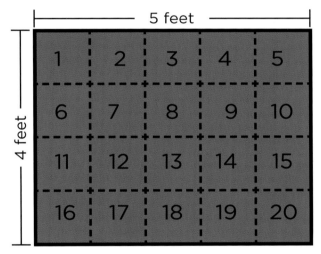

Lance needs 20 square feet of mesh.

Step 4: Review.

Does the answer match the question?
Yes. The problem asked for a number of square feet.

Can you solve this problem another way? **You can find the area of a rectangle by multiplying the length (height) by the width.**

Area of rectangle = length × width
Area of rectangle = 4 feet × 5 feet
Area of rectangle = 20 square feet

⑱ Parallelogram Area

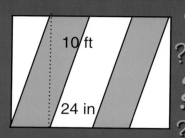

Janice is painting a mural. The background is slanted stripes, as shown on the right. To buy paint, she must know how many square feet she will be covering. What is the area of one stripe?

10 ft

24 in

Step 1: Understand the problem.

Read the problem. Is there anything you do not understand?

What does the problem ask you to find?
The area of one stripe.

What information do you need to solve the problem?
The shape and measurements of the stripe.

Step 2: Make a plan.

The stripes are parallelograms. Use the formula for the area of a parallelogram.

A formula is a mathematical rule that is written using symbols or general terms.

Parallelogram Pieces

You can cut any parallelogram perpendicular to a side and rearrange the pieces to form a rectangle.

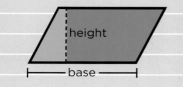

**Area of parallelogram =
base x height, or _bh_**

**Area of rectangle =
length x width, or _lw_**

Step 3: Follow the plan.

Write the formula.
Substitute the values you know.

**Area of parallelogram =
    base × height
Area of parallelogram =
    10 ft × 24 in**

Measurements must be in the same units before they are multiplied. Convert 24 inches to 2 feet.

**Area of parallelogram = 10 ft × 2 ft
Area of parallelogram = 20 ft^2**

Operations on measurements that are the same type (two lengths, two weights) must use the same units. For example, only multiply inches by inches, or feet by feet. Do NOT multiply feet by inches.

One stripe has an area of 20 square feet.

Step 4: Review.

Does the answer match the question?
Yes. The problem asks for the area of one stripe.

Did you use the correct units?
Yes. Area is always in square units. Inches were converted to feet, so the answer is in square feet.

⑲ Triangle Area

? This diagram shows a section of a protected woodland that is being studied. About how many square kilometers are in the section?

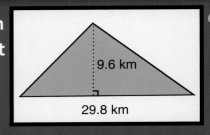

9.6 km

29.8 km

Step 1: Understand the problem.

Read the problem. Is there anything you do not understand?

What does the problem ask you to find?
The approximate area of the section of woodland shown.

What information do you need to solve the problem?
The shape and measurements of the section.

The Triangle Area Formula

Area of triangle = 1/2 (base x height), or 1/2 _bh. Why is this?_
You can take any triangle, make an exact copy of it, and form a parallelogram. The base and height of the parallelogram are the same as the base and height of the original triangle. So, since the area of the parallelogram is **base x height, the area of a triangle is half of that.**

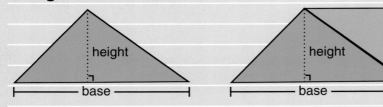

height

height

base

base

Area of triangle =
1/2 (base x height), or 1/2 _bh_

Area of parallelogram =
base x height, or _bh_

Step 2: Make a plan.

This problem does not ask for an exact area. Use the formula for the area of a triangle to estimate the area of the section.

Step 3: Follow the plan.

Write the formula. Substitute in the values you know.

Area of triangle = 1/2 (base × height)
Area of triangle = 1/2 (29.8 km × 9.6 km)

Round each of the measurements to the nearest whole kilometer. Then multiply.

Area of triangle = 1/2 (30 km × 10 km)
Area of triangle = 1/2 (300 km^2)
Area of triangle = 150 km^2

The section has an area of about 150 square kilometers.

Step 4: Review.

Does the answer match the question?
Yes. The problem asks for an estimated area.

Check the exact answer using a calculator.
Is your estimate close?
Using a calculator,
Area = 1/2 (29.8 km × 9.6 km)
= 143.04 km^2.
The estimate is close.

43

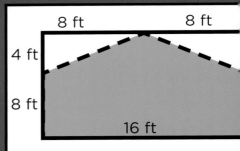

A prop for a summer camp play is cut from a sheet of cardboard. The green shape is shown in the diagram. What is the area of the shape?

Step 1: Understand the problem.

Read the problem. Is there anything you do not understand?

What does the problem ask you to find?
The area of the cut-out shape.

Is all of the information that you need in the question?
Yes, the problem gives you a diagram with measurements.

Step 2: Make a plan.

The cut-out shape is a combination of a rectangle and a triangle. You can break the shape into smaller polygons. Find the area of each polygon and add to find the total area.

Step 3: Follow the plan.

The rectangular section is 16 feet wide and 8 feet high. Use the area formula for a rectangle.

Area of rectangle = length × width
Area of rectangle = 16 feet × 8 feet
Area of rectangle = 128 square feet

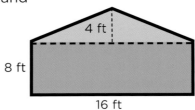

The triangular section is 16 feet wide and 4 feet high. Use the area formula for a triangle.

Area of triangle = 1/2 (base × height)
Area of triangle = 1/2 (16 feet × 4 feet)
Area of triangle = 1/2 (64 square feet)
Area of triangle = 32 square feet

Add the two sections.

Area of rectangle + area of triangle = total area
128 square feet + 32 square feet = 160 square feet

The shape has an area of 160 square feet.

Step 4: Review.

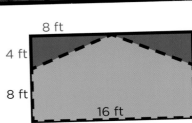

Does the answer match the question?
Yes. The problem asked for a measurement of area.

Is there another way you could solve this problem?
Yes. You could find the area of the large rectangle and subtract the area of the two small triangles that are cut away.

Area of large rectangle = 16 feet × 12 feet
Area of large rectangle = 192 square feet

Area of each small triangle =
1/2 (8 feet × 4 feet)
Area of each small triangle = 1/2 (32 square feet)
Area of each small triangle = 16 square feet

Area of large rectangle - area of two small triangles = total area
192 square feet — 2 (16 square feet) = total area
192 square feet — 32 square feet = 160 square feet

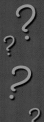

A mountain board is a skateboard with four wheels that extend beyond the board. Eric's mountain board has 34 inches between the front and back tire axles. Each tire has a radius of 3 inches. What is the total length of the mountain board?

Step 1: Understand the problem.

Read the problem. What does the problem ask you to find?
The total length of the mountain board.

What information do you need to solve the problem?
The tire sizes, the distance between the axles, and an understanding of radius.

Is all of the information that you need in the question? **Yes.**

Step 2: Make a plan.

A picture can help you understand the problem. Use the picture to decide what computations are needed.

Step 3: Follow the plan.

Draw a circle for a front tire, and a circle for a back tire. The center of the circles represents the point where the axles meet the tires. Label the measurements that you know. You know the radius of each tire and the distance between the two axles.

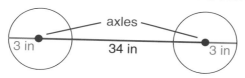

Add the radius of each tire to the length between the axles to find the total length.

front tire radius + **length between axles** + **back tire radius** = **total length**

3 in + 34 in + 3 in = 40 in

The mountain board is 40 inches long in all.

....

Step 4: Review.

Does the answer match the question? **Yes. The problem asks for total length.**

Check your math. Try adding the values in a different order. **3 in + 3 in + 34 in = 40 in**

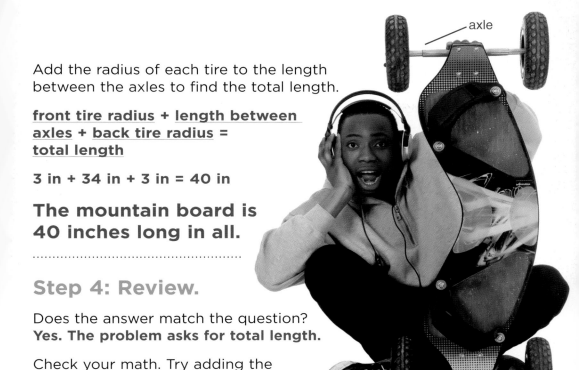

axle

axle

Circle Terms

A **circle** is a curved set of points that are all the same distance from a **center** point.

A line segment from the center to any point on the circle is called a **radius**.

center

radius

A **diameter** is a line segment that has both endpoints on the circle, and passes through the center.

diameter

㉒ Pi and Circumference

? The shape of a snare drum head is a circle. The diameter of the drum head is 28 centimeters. What is the circumference? Use 22/7 for π.

Step 1: Understand the problem.

Read the problem. What is a circumference?
The perimeter of a circle is called the circumference.

What does the problem ask you to find?
The circumference of the drum head.

What information do you need to solve the problem?
The radius or diameter of the drum head.

The ratio of the circumference to the diamete C/d, is the same for any circ

The ratio (C/d) is represented the Greek letter π, read as "p

π is approximately equal to 3.14 or 22/7.

Step 2: Make a plan.

Use the formula for the circumference of a circle.

Step 3: Follow the plan.

The formula for the circumference of a circle is $C = \pi d$ where d is the diameter or $C = 2\pi r$ where r is the radius. The information in this problem includes the diameter, so use the formula that includes diameter.

Circumference = π × diameter

Replace π with 22/7 and d with 28 cm. Since 22/7 is not an exact value for π, use the symbol for approximately equal to, ≈, in place of the equality symbol.

Circumference ≈ 22/7 × 28 cm

$$\frac{22}{7} \times \frac{28}{1} = \frac{(22)(\overset{4}{\cancel{28}})}{(\cancel{7})(1)_{1}} = \frac{88}{1} = 88 \text{ centimeters}$$

The drum head has a circumference of approximately 88 centimeters.

Step 4: Review.

Does the answer match the question?
Yes. The problem asked for the measurement of the circumference.

This problem told you to use 22/7 for π.
Why might 22/7 be a good value
to use for this problem
instead of 3.14?
**The diameter in this
problem is 28, which
is divisible by 7.
That makes it easier
to reduce when you
multiply with the
fraction 22/7, since
the denominator
is 7.**

Circle Area

The path of a tornado shows that the vortex had a radius of 0.2 kilometers when it touched down. What was the area of the circular region of ground covered by the tornado when it touched down? Round to the nearest hundredth of a square kilometer.

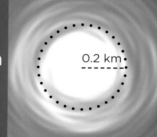

0.2 km

Step 1: Understand the problem.

Read the problem. Is there anything you do not understand?

What does the problem ask you to find?
The ground area covered by the tornado when it touched down.

What information do you need to solve the problem?
A cross section of a tornado is a circle. You need to know the measurements of that circle where the tornado touched down.

Step 2: Make a plan.

Use the formula for the area of a circle.

Step 3: Follow the plan.

The formula for the area of a circle is $A = \pi r^2$ where r is the radius.

Area of a circle = $\pi \times$ radius^2

This problem does not tell you what value to use for π. The radius is given as a decimal. The problem also asks that you round the answer to the nearest hundredth. It makes sense to use the decimal approximation for π, 3.14.

Area of a circle $\approx$ 3.14 $\times$ (0.2 km)^2
Area of a circle $\approx$ 3.14 $\times$ 0.04 km^2
Area of a circle $\approx$ 0.1256 km^2
0.1256 km^2 rounded to the nearest hundredth is 0.13 km^2

The area of the region covered by the tornado when it touched down was approximately 0.13 square kilometers.

Step 4: Review.

Does the answer match the question?
Yes. The problem asks for an area.

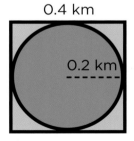

Is the answer reasonable?
Picture a square that encloses the circle. When the radius of the circle is 0.2 km, the side length of the square is 0.4 km. A square with a side length of 0.4 km has an area of 0.4 x 0.4 = 0.16 km^2. This is a little more than the answer for the area of the circle. This is reasonable, since the square has a little more area in each corner.

㉔ Similar Figures

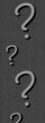

Kristen's senior picture package includes several sizes of portraits. The smallest photo is a rectangle, 1.5 inches wide and 2 inches tall. The largest photo is 9 inches wide. It has a similar shape to the smallest photo. How tall is the largest photo?

Step 1: Understand the problem.

Read the problem. What does the problem ask you to find?
The height of the largest photo.

Do you have all of the information you need to solve the problem?
Yes, you know the photos are similar figures and you know enough measurements to find the missing one.

Congruent figures have the same shape and size.

Similar figures have the same shape, but not always the same size. Corresponding angle measures are equal. Corresponding side lengths are proportional.

Step 2: Make a plan.

Set up a proportion using the ratio of width to height. Solve the proportion to find the missing height.

Step 3: Follow the plan.

Set up the proportion with a ratio of width to height on each side of the proportion. Fill in the ratios with the numbers given in the problem.

$$\frac{\text{width}}{\text{height}} = \frac{\text{width}}{\text{height}} \qquad \frac{1.5}{2} = \frac{9}{?}$$

One way to find a missing term in a proportion is to use cross multiplication. Cross multiply, then divide to find the missing term.

$$\frac{1.5}{2} = \frac{9}{?}$$

Cross multiply. $(1.5 \times ?) = (2 \times 9)$
Divide 18 ÷ 1.5. $(1.5 \times ?) = (18)$
                                    $? = \quad 18 ÷ 1.5 = 12$

The largest photo is 12 inches tall.

....

Step 4: Review.

Does the answer match the question?
Yes. The problem asked for a measurement.

Check your answer.
What can you multiply the width of the small photo by to get the width of the large photo? **To change 1.5 to 9, you multiply by a factor of 6.**

Does the height change by the same factor? **The height of the small photo, 2 inches, multiplied by 6 is 12 inches. Yes.**

53

Classify Solids

Name the three-dimensional figure represented by each object.

1.    2.    3.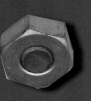

Step 1: Understand the problem.

Read the problem. What is a solid? **A solid is a figure that has three dimensions: length, width, and height. Solids are also called three-dimensional figures.**

What does the problem ask you to find?
The name for each three-dimensional figure.

What information do you need to solve the problem?
You need to have a picture or description of each object, and know the classifications of solids.

Step 2: Make a plan.

Classify each figure according to its characteristics.

Step 3: Follow the plan.

There are three figures. Look at the characteristics of each.

Figure 1 is a roll of toilet paper. It has two bases. The bases are circular.

Figure 1 is a cylinder.

Solid Classification

Solid figures with all flat surfaces are called **polyhedrons**. Polyhedrons with two congruent parallel bases are called **prisms**. Prisms are named by the shape of their bases. For example, a prism with three-sided bases is called a **triangular prism**.

Pyramids are polyhedrons with only one base. The rest of the faces are triangles that meet at a common vertex. Pyramids are also named by their base. A pyramid with an eight-sided base is called an octagonal pyramid.

Cylinders and cones are not polyhedrons. A **cylinder** has two congruent parallel bases that are circular. A **cone** has one circular base, and a curved face that comes to a point.

Figure 2 is an Eqyptian pyramid. It has one base. The base appears to be square.

Figure 2 is a square pyramid.

Figure 3 is a bolt. It has two bases. Each base is a hexagon.

Figure 3 is a hexagonal prism.

Step 4: Review.

Did you name each figure?
Yes. There are three figures. There are three answers.

Check each object. Do the objects match the description for each named figure? **Yes.**

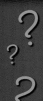

㉖ Volume

Wayne buys sugar cubes for his horse that are exactly one cubic centimeter. Each box of sugar cubes has 2 layers of sugar cubes. Each layer is 3 cubes across and 4 cubes long. Find the volume of the box in cubic centimeters.

Step 1: Understand the problem.

Read the problem. What does the problem ask you to find?
The volume of the box.

Do you have the information you need to solve the problem?
Yes. You know how many layers of sugar cubes are in a container and the dimensions of each layer.

Volume measures the amount of space a figure occupies.

Volume is measured in cubic units. Each cubic unit is one unit long, one unit wide, and one unit high. Cubic units are abbreviated as units³.

Step 2: Make a plan.

You can draw a picture to find the number of sugar cubes in a container.
Since each sugar cube is one cubic centimeter, the number of sugar cubes is the same as the number of cubic centimeters.

Step 3: Follow the plan.

Draw a set of cubes that is 3 cubes across and 4 cubes long. This is one layer of cubes. Count the number of cubes in one layer.

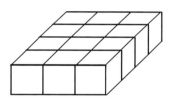

There are 12 cubes in one layer.

There are two layers of cubes. Add to find the total.

12 + 12 = 24

Each cube is one cubic centimeter. There are 24 cubes.

The volume of the box is 24 cubic centimeters.

Step 4: Review.

Does the answer match the question?
Yes. The problem asked for volume in cubic centimeters.

Is there another way you can solve this problem?
Yes. You can use multiplication. One layer of cubes is 3 cubes across and 4 cubes long. You can multiply to find the number of cubes in a layer. Then you can multiply the number of cubes in a layer by 2 to find the total.
3 × 4 × 2 = 24

Individual slices of pizza are sold in a box that is a triangular prism. The triangular base is 8 inches wide and has a height of 7 inches. The box is 2 inches tall. What is the volume of the box?

Step 1: Understand the problem.

Read the problem. Is there anything you do not understand?

What does the problem ask you to find?
The volume of the pizza box.

Do you have all of the information you need to solve the problem?
Yes. You know the dimensions of the triangular base and the height of the box.

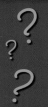

Volume Formulas

The formula for the volume of a rectangular prism is:
Volume = length × width × height, or $V = lwh$

The formula for the volume of a prism or cylinder is:
Volume = area of base × height, or $V = Bh$

In geometric formulas, a lower case b is used for the length of a side, like the base of a triangle. An uppercase B is used for the area of a base, like the base of a prism or cylinder.

Step 2: Make a plan.

Break the problem into two parts. First, find the area of the triangular base of the box. Then, use the area of the base to find the volume of the box.

....

Step 3: Follow the plan.

Write the formula for the area of the base. Substitute in the values you know.

Area of triangle base, B, = 1/2 (base × height)
Area of triangle base, B, = 1/2 (8 inches × 7 inches)
Area of triangle base, B, = 28 in^2

Write the formula for the volume of a prism. Substitute in the values you know.

Volume of a prism = area of base × height
Volume of a prism = 28 inches^2 × 2 inches
Volume of a prism = 56 in^3

The box has a volume of 56 cubic inches.

....

Step 4: Review.

Does the answer match the question?
Yes. The question asked for a volume.

Did you include the correct units in your answer?
Yes. The volume is in cubic units. This problem uses inches, so the answer is in cubic inches.

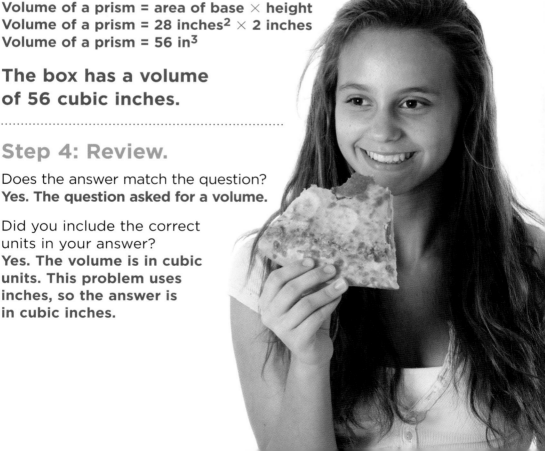

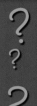 Surface Area

Two boxes with the same volume contain fudge for a fundraiser. Box A is 9 inches tall, 4 inches wide, and 3 inches deep. Box B is 9 inches tall, 6 inches wide, and 2 inches deep. Which box style has more surface area?

Step 1: Understand the problem.

Read the problem. What is surface area?
Surface area is the total of the areas of all of the faces on a solid.

What does the problem ask you to find?
Which of the two box styles has more surface area.

Do you have all of the information you need to solve the problem?
Yes. You know the measurements of each box.

Step 2: Make a plan.

Draw a sketch of each box to understand the measurements.

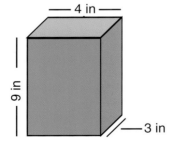
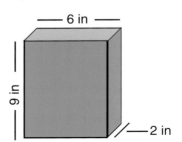

Use an organized table to keep track of the area on each face of the boxes and the surface area. Compare the surface areas.

Step 3: Follow the plan.

Each box is a rectangular prism. A rectangular prism has 6 faces. Find the surface area by adding the area of each face. There are three different-sized faces, with two of each size. Let's look the different faces.

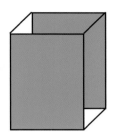 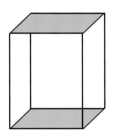 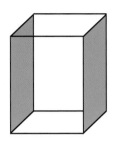

Area of rectangle = length × width	Box A	Box B
Front and Back	$9 \times 4 = 36$ in^2	$9 \times 6 = 54$ in^2
Top and Bottom	$4 \times 3 = 12$ in^2	$6 \times 2 = 12$ in^2
Sides	$9 \times 3 = 27$ in^2	$9 \times 2 = 18$ in^2
Surface Area = sum of two of each size face	36 + 36 + 12 + 12 + 27 + 27 = 150 in^2	54 + 54 + 12 + 12 + 18 + 18 = 168 in^2

Box A has a surface area of 150 in^2.
Box B has a surface area of 168 in^2.

Box B has more surface area.

Step 4: Review.

Is there another way you can solve this problem?
Yes. You could draw a net for each box to find the surface area. A net is a drawing of what the box would look like if you cut it apart along its edges and laid it flat. Find the area of the flat net.

Further Reading

Books

The Math Forum, Drexel University. *Dr. Math Introduces Geometry: Learing Geometry is Easy! Just Ask Dr. Math!* Hoboken, N.J.: Wiley, 2004.

School Speciality Publishing. *The Complete Book of Math.* Grand Rapids, Mich.: School Speciality Publishing, 2001.

More Math Help from Rebecca Wingard-Nelson:

Wingard-Nelson, Rebecca. *Figuring Out Geometry.* Berkeley Heights, N.J.: Enslow Publishers, Inc., 2008.

Internet Addresses

Banfill, J. *AAA Math.* "Geometry." © 2009.
<http://www.aaaknow.com/geo.html>

Math Is Fun. "Geometry." © 2009.
<http://www.mathsisfun.com/geometry/index.html>

The Math Forum. "Ask Dr. Math." © 1994–2010.
<http://mathforum.org/library/drmath/sets/elem_division.html>

Index